Take Your Feet Off The Seat

Respect Leadership

I0081338

Bishop Rosette Coney

www.gospel4unetwork.com

ISBN - 9780692609675
Library of Congress Control
Number: 2016930220

Printed in United States of America
January 2016

Content

DEDICATION

FOREWORD

FOREWORD

ACKNOWLEDGEMENT

INTRODUCTION

1. Identifying the "Seat" 17

2. Attributes of a Leader......................................23

3. Respect the Seat..37

4. Touch Not My Anointed.................................. 43

5. Obey the One in the Seat................................. 51

6. Don't Get Caught in the Mouth Trap...............61

7. Don't Kill the Shepherd....................................67

8. Giving Honor to the Seat.................................85

9. Misery Loves Company.....................................93

10. Leaders Go Through Too.................................99

11. Remember, You Get Back What You Give.....107

12. Appreciating a Leader Who's On Fire.............114

13. Learning to Accept a New Leader...................121

14. Never Forget Them...127

Prayer of Repentance

Encouraging Words from Bishop Coney

Dedication

This book is dedicated to all leaders - great and small, and to those they serve in the spirit of humility and love.

Foreword

This erudite, eloquent, and immensely thought-provoking word gets to the heart of one of the most important aspects of true leadership. It is indispensable reading for all progressive leaders who want to serve at a level of excellence in the church. This is a profound, authoritative work, spanning the wisdom of the ages, and yet breaking new ground in its approach in a way that is both unique and creative.

This exceptional work by Bishop Rosette Coney is one of the most profound, practical principle-centered approaches to this subject I have read in a long time. In can't remember the last time I turned the pages of a book so eagerly. Bishop Coney's words have revolutionized my way of thinking about respect for leadership in the church. The author is remarkably gifted at explaining universal heart truths to those who serve as leaders. She will challenge you to examine "how" and "why" you serve. Reading *Take Your Feet Off The Seat* is like having your own personal mentor by your side as you pursue God's assignment on your life.

Every chapter of this book is filled with extraordinary information. I encourage you to plunge into this ocean of wisdom and knowledge. Allow Bishop Coney to encourage and equip you, remembering that our service is ultimately "unto the Lord."

Bishop Millicent Hunter, Ed.D., D. Min.

Worship Center Worldwide Fellowship of Churches

Foreword

Leadership, "the ability to inspire others to perform tasks that help to accomplish a corporate goal". With this thought in mind, Bishop Rosette Coney has taken a step to inspire those with principles of Biblical Leadership.

"Take Your Feet Off The Seat" is designed to create a healthy view of Biblical Leadership and encourage those who serve leaders. Our church experiences often prevent us from following our leaders with true humility. We must remember that the Lord encourages us to respect our leaders, honor our leaders, and obey our leaders.

Bishop Rosette Coney is a true Biblical Leader, and she imparts that knowledge and grace to the readers. The principles that Bishop Coney shares are rooted in the Word of God and come from her many years of serving the Kingdom of God as a leader. She not only encourages those who lead through her personal example, but she has also served her leaders well.

When you read this book, you will find encouragement and humility to serve others in the Spirit of Christ, and you will gain a new appreciation for those who you may lead. This book will also encourage those who serve leaders and bring them a new appreciation for that responsibility. I pray that you will enjoy this book and find some principles to apply to your everyday life.

Grace and Peace to all.

Bishop Eric A. Lambert, Jr.

Presiding Bishop

Bethel Deliverance International Fellowship of Churches, Inc.

Acknowledgements

First and foremost, I acknowledge the Almighty God, who allowed me the privilege of serving under great leaders for most of my life. I served them with joy and with passion, because He placed that spirit inside of me.

Included in the ranks of great leaders, is my dedicated husband, Gene, who have led my household since 1971, with wisdom, patience, support and love; to my two daughters, Tamika and Anitra, who allowed me to lead them into becoming wonderful wives to their husbands and loving mothers to my beautiful grandchildren (Makayla, Tamia and Aaron); to my two sisters, Faye and Sharon – your love and prayers sustained me.

To all of my spiritual children and congregation who have followed my leadership and guidance down through the years – I love you for that!

To the one component that I practiced leadership skills on daily, Sara, and who never left my side through it all.

To the great deceased leaders who impacted my life in a tremendous way: The late Reverend H. C. Williams (grandfather), the late Bishop M. L. Jewell, the late Dr. N. A. Manning, the Late Bishop Ninious Randall, and the late Bishop Elleree Coney. I miss you!

To the awesome current leaders of whom I honor and love dearly: Bishop Faye Moore, Bishop Tony Harley, Bishop Millicent Hunter and Bishop Eric A. Lambert. I carry within my heart a nugget of wisdom from each of you, and will acknowledge your leadership roles in my life for as long as I live! I appreciate each of you for supporting and inspiring me to write this book.

Thank you!

Introduction

*This book is for the purpose of returning us to the plan established by God many years ago – obedience to **leadership; His** first, and then to those he set to lead his people as they were inspired by Him.*

Today, a church's or organization's survival and success depend on one word:

"LEADERSHIP"

Leadership is the skill that matters most in today's fast-paced, high-pressure world. The pastors and leaders who obey the leading of the Holy Spirit and his divine order will prosper. Those who choose not to obey will fail. It's as simple as that.

Traditionally, leadership has involved motivating, guiding, training, inspiring, building up, empowering, advising, managing, controlling, organizing, and authorizing. In times past, individuals not possessing these traits would have been disqualified as a leader.

But the role of the leader is changing. The old

command-and-control model is crumbling. New definitions are taking its place such as: strategist, coach, facilitator, cheerleader, mediator, team-builder. Leaders need to know how to work smarter – not harder; and those being led need to know how to follow faithfully and with dedication.

Leadership is not to make anyone feel like they are sub servant or slaves to any human being, but to comply with the established set of guidelines already set in order, which will place us in the position of being blessed in all areas of our lives.

This book will allow readers to take a look at how their respect of leadership can be enhanced and for other readers, how their skills of following leadership can be upgraded!

From a dedicated follower's perspective, and passionate leader's perspective; I pray that it will be a blessing to anyone who takes the time to add it to their collection of inspiring publications.

Bishop Rosette Coney
Senior Pastor, Church of the Living God

Bishop Rosette Coney

#1 IDENTIFYING THE SEAT

The **SEAT** represents the Leader –

- The authority figure
- The one in charge
- The manager
- The trailblazer
- The head
- The principal
- The organizer
- The chief
- The boss
- The director

All of the above mentioned images spell out the person of responsibility leading others. Those who occupy the above seats, often lead with an authoritative, skillful, and wise perspective of the tasks at hand. Knowing what, when, where, and how to make sound decisions, involves much wisdom.

One may ask, "well, what is wisdom" and "where does it come from? The answer to both of these questions is simply this: **"Wisdom is both the ability to discern what is best and the strength of character to act upon that knowledge".**, It does not come from a college degree; it does not come from work experience; it does not come from reading a lot of books, although one can gain earthly wisdom and knowledge from engaging such things ; **but, true wisdom that is from above, comes from the all-knowing, all-powerful, all-mighty Creator and Lord of all, our God -** *HE* **is wisdom and** *HE* **is where all true wisdom comes from.** Being a know-it-all certainly is not a sign of wisdom. Believe it or not, nobody knows it all! Only God knows it all because He is **Omniscient**. This wisdom can only be acquired by simply seeking it from God. Proverbs 2:6 reads, *"For the LORD giveth wisdom: out of his mouth cometh knowledge and understanding."*

18

A good and wise leader is identified by his or her fear of The LORD; and his or her ability to recognize their insignificance, in comparison to the all knowing and all wise God our Savior.

AFTER THOUGHT

This is where it's safe to put your feet, once you've identified the Seat...

It's safe to place your feet in motion to be of assistance to your pastor or leader once you have identified the seat. You must understand the responsibility of carrying the torch to lead is not an easy task. Leaders have people in their care who have needs spiritually, physically, mentally, and emotionally. If you busy yourself offering assistance to them while they are carrying these heavy loads, you will avoid falling into the category of walking all over their seat. Just as the leaders have a responsibility to care for the people – the people have a responsibility to respect and honor their leaders.

In identifying the seat, you must be aware of the weight placed upon the one who sits on the seat. You allow your foot prints to tread lightly even around the area of the seat. You become cautious of what you say and how you give reverence to the position. In doing so, you will save yourself a lot of grief and hardship.

> **"Let the elders that rule well be counted worthy of double honor, especially they who labor in the word and doctrine**
>
> **1Timothy 5:17**

Double honor is not only defined as supporting your leader financially, but most importantly, esteeming your leader for the very office that they hold. That is what is known as double honor!

How can you show your leader that you recognize their seat?

#2 ATTRIBUTES OF A GOOD LEADER

In order for a good leader to be recognized as such, they must demonstrate certain attributes that cause others to follow them. I share the following attributes with you that undeniably mark those who are truly good leaders:

What others see in them...

Confidence: Leaders walk in full assurance of the impossibility for God to fail them at anything. *"For with God nothing shall be impossible" (Luke 1:37).*

Faith: Leaders are fully persuaded in the existence of God and His ability to lead them and provide the wisdom needed for them to lead

23

others. *"But without faith it is impossible to please him: for he that cometh to God must believe that he is, and that he is a rewarder of them that diligently seek him"* (Hebrews 11:6).

Diligence: Leaders are laborious in the tasks at hand,_*"Seest thou a man diligent in his business? He shall stand before kings; he shall not stand before mean men"* (Proverbs 22:29).

Lowliness: Leaders rule with humility, they present themselves before God and man with devoted servitude, they take this as their reasonable responsibility. *"I beseech you therefore, brethren, by the mercies of God, that ye present your bodies a living sacrifice, holy, acceptable unto God, which is your reasonable service"* (Romans 12:1).

Strength of character: Leaders do not become visibly ruffled or irritated when someone raises an objection, questions their authority or change programs without notifying them. *"Wherefore seeing we also are compassed about with so great a cloud of witnesses, let us lay aside every weight,* *and the sin which doth so easily beset us, and let us run with patience the race that is set before us" (Hebrews 12:1).*

<u>Vigilance:</u> Leaders possess a watchful eye when caring for those they lead. They are in full control and are aware of their surroundings at all times. *"Be sober, be vigilant; because your adversary the devil, as a roaring lion, walketh about, seeking whom he may devour:" (1st Peter 5:8).*

Leaders mind their words

<u>Speak distinctly:</u> And loudly enough to be heard by all – yet their speech is with wisdom and love. *"My mouth shall speak of wisdom; and the meditation of my heart shall be of understanding" (Psalm 49:3).*

<u>Conscientious:</u> About what they say in a crowd. They never know who is listening. *"Be not forgetful to entertain strangers: for thereby some have entertained angels unawares" (Hebrews 13:2).*

Exercise integrity: What they know is factual, and not what was rumored. *"Whereunto I am ordained a preacher, and an apostle, I speak the truth in Christ, and lie not; a teacher of the Gentiles in faith and verity" (1st Timothy 2:7).*

***Build* friendly Relationships with others**: They lead without lording, direct without dictating, and counsel without criticizing. *"And the fruit of righteousness is sown in peace of them that make peace" (James 3:18).*

***Delegate* their Responsibility:** They realize that this is not a "one-man show". They recognize that the lone-ranger flavor is counter-productive. *"Two are better than one; because they have a good reward for their labor" (Ecclesiastes 4:9).*

Teach ideas and Visions: Transferring them to the hearts and minds of others. *"And the LORD answered me, and said, Write the vision, and make it plain upon tables, that he may run that* *readeth it" (Habakkuk 2:2).*

Not easily Intimidated: By others who are under them and appear to know more than they do. They celebrate the achievement and successes of the people they inspire. *"Verily, verily, I say unto you, He that believeth on me, the works that I do shall he do also; and greater works than these shall he do; because I go unto my Father"* (John 14:12).

They have a good attitude...

Attitude of leaders determine their altitude: *"For whosoever exalteth himself shall be abased; and he that humbleth himself shall be exalted" (Luke 14:11).*

Sincere and enthusiastic: their enthusiasm captures others so they are eager to cooperate. *"Not slothful in business; fervent in spirit; serving the Lord" (Rom 12:11).*

Open minded: they welcome new ideas, use

them where ever they are appropriate and timely; give credit where it is due. *"Render therefore to all their dues: tribute to whom tribute is due; custom to whom custom; fear to whom fear; honor to whom honor" (Rom 13:7).*

Think positively: regardless of how bleak the circumstances and situations are. *"Unto the pure all things are pure: but unto them that are defiled and unbelieving is nothing pure; but even their mind and conscience is defiled" (Titus 1:15).*

Have a spirit of humility: they are dependent upon God for wisdom, power and fruitfulness. They publicly and privately give God praise, glory and honor. *"Likewise, ye younger, submit yourselves unto the elder. Yea, all of you be subject one to another, and be clothed with humility: for God resisteth the proud, and giveth grace to the humble. Humble yourselves therefore under the mighty hand of God, that he may exalt you in due time" (1st Peter 5:5-6).*

Leaders realize their power comes from

an Omnipotent God...

They are fully persuaded he alone liberates, elevates, educates, compensates, motivates, regenerates, and activates them to lead people with success.

- **God by his Spirit liberates**: He frees them from the chains, stains, and pains of their past mistakes.
- **God by his Spirit elevates**: He embraces them and lifts them up to reign with Him.
- **God by his Spirit educates**: He gives them wise counsel, future direction and knowledge through his Holy Word.
- **God by his Spirit compensates**: He fills up areas where they are weak or lack competence with his love and grace.
- **God by his Spirit motivates**: He becomes their source of vision, hope, and purpose.
- **God by his Spirit regenerates**: He transforms them to live on a higher level with his supernatural resources.

o **God by his Spirit activates**: He commissions them to obey and move forward in His cause by allowing His Holy Spirit to speak to their spirits.

They are relational...

To better understand the word relational, look at the root word - relate. Relate is linked to the following terms:

o Connect (unite)
o Associate (partner; fellow worker)
o Correlate (show a relationship)
o Join (bond; stick together)
o Attach (put together)
o Interact (intermingle; work together)
o Cooperate (assist; help; lend a hand)

Great leaders relate to others horizontally and vertically: They respond to and respect those over them, as well as those who work directly under them.

A relationship is a partnership: Apostle Paul

teaches in 1st Corinthians 1:10, *"Now I plead with you, brethren, by the name of our Lord Jesus Christ, that you all speak the same thing, and that there be no divisions among you, but that you be perfectly joined together in the same mind and in the same judgment."* Now, that's a relationship!

Great leaders connect themselves with ships that are going somewhere: Ships docked in one spot cannot advance forward.

Good leaders create a unified corporate atmosphere: The corporate objectives and goals are communicated to all, making them aware of the fact that they are all working on the same team and everyone should be pulling in the same direction (Amos 3:3).

Relationships are built upon good communication skills: Success is never achieved playing guessing games. Clear concise communication is vital and can eliminate problems and ward off negative chains of reaction.

Leaders relate to others by mastering the art of one-anothering: It is a fact that people do not care how much leaders know until they know how much leaders care. Leaders cannot separate leadership from relationship. Much can be learned from Apostle Paul's theory on developing good relationships (Roman 12:9-21).

Relationships are Rewarding: Building relationships with others allow leaders to reach their goals. The rewards of a healthy relationship are:
- Ability to accomplish more
- One completes the other
- One can comfort and support the other
- One can strengthen the other

"Two are better than one; because they have a good reward for their labour" **(Eccl. 4:9).**

AFTER THOUGHT

Displayed Attributes Will Help You Keep Your Feet Off the Seat...

When you serve under a leader who takes their job seriously, it is much easier to respect their seat and not walk all over them. However, if they take advantage of their position and also those who serve under them, it is not the subordinate's job to challenge their leader – God will manifest his position on the situation and handle it accordingly. He is God and very much on top of his game.

If your leader displays good and positive attributes, let your feet walk in the direction of working under them with the best of your ability – in humility and with sincerity. If they display negative characteristics, you are still responsible, in the sight of God, to serve them faithfully. Let God handle the matter, and you will be free of guilt.

> *"Servants, be obedient to them that are your masters according to the flesh, with fear and trembling,*
> *in singleness of your heart, as unto Christ;"*
> *Ephesians 6:5*
>
> *"Servants, be subject to your masters with all fear; not only to the good and gentle, but also to the froward."*
> *1st Peter 2:18*

What attributes impact you most about your leader?

#3 RESPECT THE SEAT!

David respected Saul's seat...

1st Samuel 24:1-15 tells the story of how David had an opportunity to destroy Saul, who at this time was the King. David knew that Saul was out to destroy him, yet he had so much respect for leadership that he passed up the tempting opportunity to destroy Saul and spared his life. He recognized the fact that Saul, however bad he had gotten, was still anointed by God to be king—and David would respect him no matter what. David knew that **God** was the Avenger. He dared not put his feet on the seat.

There may be poor leaders in our lives – those who demonstrate the lack of wisdom, and even some who are obnoxious in every way – but we are still saddled with the responsibility of obedience to God by honoring them.

David had yet another opportunity to slay Saul, as recorded in 1st Samuel 26—but he said to Abishai his accomplice, *"Don't destroy him; who can lay a hand on the Lord's anointed and be guiltless? As surely as the Lord lives,"* he said, *"the Lord Himself will strike him...But the Lord forbid that I should lay a hand on the Lord's anointed."*

You must continually respect the seat...

There may be occasions in your life where you actually know more about a matter than your superior. Your best bet would be to address the matter in a respectable way – not looking to shame your leader or belittle them – but merely to enlighten them appropriately.

It is always in the best of everyone's interest to

create a "win-win" situation than to destroy a leader/subordinate relationship.

The law of reciprocity will place you in a position, as you live on, to reap what you sow (Gal 6:7). Spare yourself the embarrassment by honoring and respecting your "not-knowing-it-all leader, just in case a similar circumstance creeps up in your life with someone you preside over in the future.

"Abandon your desire to walk all over your pastor or leader — take your feet off the seat!"

AFTER THOUGHT

Respect Your Leader and Keep Your Feet Off the Seat...

You may not personally like the head of the team, but you are required to honor and respect the seat they occupy. David was chased by his leader, who became quite jealous of him. David had to run for his life, but he feared God enough to restrain himself from bringing harm to this vicious leader called Saul, who sought to end his life. Even when the opportunity was presented to him – he confined himself to the will of God.

Let's review this portion of David's story as recorded in 1st Samuel 24:4-6:

"4And the men of David said unto him, Behold the day of which the LORD said unto thee, Behold, I will deliver thine enemy into thine hand, that thou mayest do to him as it shall seem good unto thee. Then David arose, and cut off the skirt of Saul's robe privily. 5And it came to pass afterward, that David's heart

smote him, because he had cut off Saul's skirt. *⁶And he said unto his men, The LORD forbid that I should do this thing unto my master, the LORD's anointed, to stretch forth mine hand against him, seeing he is the anointed of the LORD"* (1 Samuel 24:4-6).

It has been said by many that respect has to be earned, but I rise to differ with that – God requires us to honor and respect those who have rule over us; and it is not contingent upon their behavior – good or bad. We have to respect the seat.

> *"Honor all men. Love the brotherhood.*
>
> *Fear God. Honor the king."*
>
> 1ˢᵗ Peter 2:17

What can you practice doing to show more respect for your leader?

#4 TOUCH NOT MY ANOINTED!

How do you touch the anointed ones?

When you put your hands on something that does not belong to you; take possession of what does not belong to you; or involve yourself in another man's matters; you have touched them – physically, spiritually, emotionally and or mentally.

It doesn't matter whether your pastor, leader, supervisor or manager, is *in your eyes* right or wrong. The fact remains that they are elected, selected and anointed by God to do the work assigned to their hands. If something isn't right, God Himself will handle it. In the corporate world, everyone has a boss or leader over them; and it is their responsibility to set things in order.

Let everyone be subject to the governing authorities, for there is no authority except that which have been established by God. The authorities that exist have been established by God. Consequently, whoever rebels against the authority is rebelling against what God has instituted, and those who do so will bring judgment on themselves (Romans 13:10). (NIV)

Curses placed on individuals who defy the orders of God can be a travesty for them and their entire household. Just look at what happened to those who tried to rebel against the leadership of Moses and Aaron in Numbers the 16th chapter. The anger of the Lord kindled to destroy several families of those leaders.

And it came to pass, as he had made an end of speaking all these words, that the ground clave asunder that was under them: And the earth opened her mouth, and swallowed them up, and their houses, and all the men that appertained unto Korah, and all their goods. They, and all that appertained to them, went down alive into the pit, and the earth closed upon them; and they perished from among the congregation **(Num16:31-33).**

It's dangerous to touch the Leaders...

God put individuals over you for a specific purpose, and at the appointed time (*His time*) he will take them away from their positions. That's not your responsibility.

1st Chronicles 16:22 and **Psalm 105:15** read, *"...Touch not mine anointed, and do my prophets no harm."* Those who have been placed in a leadership role by God are a protected class. God uses people here on earth to accomplish great tasks from the heavenly realm. He uses their hands, their mouths, their hearts and their feet. They speak his words – they lay hands on people to produce his healing – they go into areas where he sends them to change for some the course of destruction and give direction to those who have lost their way.

Adonijah thought that he would become king over Solomon, bragging and boasting well before King David had even passed away. Adonijah felt pretty bad when David anointed Solomon to be the next king. Ultimately, Solomon had to have Adonijah put to death on the grounds that, by seeking to marry David's concubine Abishag, he was aiming at the crown **(1 Kings 2:22-24).** He lost his life in the attempt to put his feet on the seat.

Truly it is not worth it; and actually, it's easier to follow rather than lead. Leading carries with it a greater responsibility than following. Good and faithful leaders are birthed from good and faithful followers.

Solomon was fortunate enough to have a loving mother who spoke up for him when the enemy was seeking to slide in over him **(1Kings 15-40).** What God intends to happen, happens without fail. This should encourage those who feel they've been passed over for promotions or positions in leadership. There should be no worry when your faith and trust is in God. Romans 8:28 reminds us of the fact that all things will work in our favor if we love the Lord..... "And we know that in all things God works for the good of those who love him, who have been called according to his purpose."

In the process of waiting for your time to come, you must still be in control of your emotions and your actions. You cannot touch God's anointed ones verbally, or physically. Of course, this is easier said than done, but the decision to do things this way can only be accomplished by those who want to do what is right in the sight of the LORD.

Touch not my anointed is a command given by God, and therefore, must be followed without compromise.

Adonijah's fate was sealed when he decided to walk all over his leader/father and self-appoint himself as the next leader, while his leader was near death.

AFTER THOUGHT

Don't Touch the Seat, With Your Hands or Your Feet...

There are a lot of things you can touch without risk of great retribution, but touching someone whom God has anointed for His own purpose comes with a price that you may not be able to pay.

God is very sensitive about his leaders, and he protects them at all costs. God uses his leaders in accomplishing his work here on earth. Through them, He impacts the entire world.

One of the most thought provoking scriptures depicting the seriousness of this immeasurable offense, is King Jeroboam who was smitten by The Lord when he stretched forth his hand against the prophet sent by God:

> *"4 And it came to pass, when king Jeroboam heard the saying of the man of God, which had cried against the altar in Bethel, that he put forth his hand from the altar, saying, Lay hold on him. And his hand, which he put forth against him, dried up, so that he could not pull it in again to him. 5 The altar also was rent, and the ashes poured out from the altar, according to the sign which the man of God had given by the word of the LORD."*
>
> 1st Kings 13:4-5

What dangers could you face in coming against God's anointed leader?

Bishop Rosette Coney

#5 OBEY THE ONE IN THE SEAT!

Hebrews 13:17 instructs us to obey our leaders and submit to their authority. They are responsible for watching over us and giving account for our souls. We should obey them to make their jobs one of joy and not of burden, for that would be of no advantage to us.

Reading the story in 1 Samuel 24 will encourage you not to rise up against your leader...

As a matter of fact, you should practice covering up your leaders' weaknesses – they are human beings just like you, and God chose them for a reason, for a purpose and for a time. Remember that God will judge those who are over you – just like He will judge you if you do not obey them.

51

Please do not pray selfishly for God to straighten out someone who you feel has wronged you while under their authority; unless you are willing for him to straighten you out for your wrong doing first. Some people pride themselves in seeking revenge on those who have rule over them by verbally ripping apart their character and reputation to others. When you find a person constantly tearing down their leaders, in most cases a spirit of offense, rebellion, envy and or jealousy is at work! The word of God gives clear direction on how to handle such cases (Psalm 37).

Lets take the strongest of these; which is rebellion for example...

Rebellion is never a good position to occupy. The Bible strictly warns us against taking such a stand. It is a clear indication that your heart is not right with God. Notice *Psalms 78:8, "And might not be as their fathers, a stubborn and rebellious generation; a generation that set not their* heart aright, and whose spirit was not steadfast with God."

Notice Ezekiel 12:2, "Son of man, thou dwellest in the midst of a rebellious house, which have eyes to see, and see not; they have ears to hear, and hear not: for they are a rebellious house."In this state you are cut off from God.   Satan works through his network of demonic spirits to blind your spiritual eyes, ears, and perception. When your spiritual eyesight is blinded, your discernment suffers greatly.   It can become hard for you to hear God when He tries to speak to you, thereby putting your vision at risk.

The Word of God declares that rebellion is in the same category of sin as witchcraft. Notice 1 Samuel 15:23, "For rebellion is as the sin of witchcraft..."

The word witchcraft is similar to divination. Both of these practices are demonic. Individuals possessing these traits, can become a real problem for a leader. God will bring destruction upon any of his people who decide to turn their backs on Him to practice this evil craft. Notice **2 Kings 17:16-18,"** *And they left all the commandments of the LORD their God, and made them molten images, ent two calves, and made a grove, and worshiped all the host of heaven, and served Baal. And they caused their sons and their daughters to pass through the fire, and used divination and enchantments, and sold themselves to do evil in the sight of the LORD, to provoke him to anger. Therefore the Lord was very angry with Israel, and removed them out of his sight: there was none left but the tribe of Judah only. And the LORD rejected all the seed of Israel, and afflicted them and delivered them into the hand of spoilers, until he had cast them out of his sight.* And this is what led to the demise of such a great nation of whom The LORD led with a cloud by day and fire by night; all because of Rebellion! If your rebellion can lead to *your demise, then truly your obedience can lead to your success!*

Your obedience will produce your overall prosperity...

Deuteronomy 28 gives a powerful list of *"if you wills"*, *"then you will haves."* It also lists the *"if you will nots", including* a list of curses for disobedience. If you have the willingness to obey your leaders, you have the power to have whatever you need.

Even if you don't understand what you're asked to do by your pastor or leader — you will be blessed through your spirit of obedience. Look at what happened to the widow woman of Zarephath who, during a famine in the land, obeyed the Prophet Elijah's instructions to provide food for him **first**, and then for her and her starving son. Through her immediate obedience, her barrel went into the overflow mode (1st Kings 17:13-16).

"13And Elijah said unto her, Fear not; go and do as thou hast said: but make me thereof a little cake first, and bring it unto me, and after

make for thee and for thy son. 14 For thus saith the Lord God of Israel, The barrel of meal shall not waste, neither shall the cruse of oil fail, until the day that the Lord sendeth rain upon the earth. 15 And she went and did according to the saying of Elijah: and she, and he, and her house, did eat many days. 16 And the barrel of meal wasted not, neither did the cruse of oil fail, according to the word of the Lord, which he spake by Elijah."

Your instructions or orders may seem to be a bit off base at times, but if you ever want to experience success, you've got to follow those orders—even if you have to pray to God as you go along.   Prayer will help you bare the toil and endure the pain, as you build yourself up in God's Word.

My sisters and brothers,

when you obey

Your life will be blessed

in every way!

(Deuteronomy 28)

"Obey them that have the rule over you, and submit yourselves: for they watch for your souls, as they that must give account, that they may do it with joy, and not with grief: for that is unprofitable for you."

— Hebrews 13:17

AFTER THOUGHT

Obedience will keep your feet where they are supposed to be...

There may be many occasions when a leader will give a directive that isn't palatable to the subordinate. If there is a disagreement, there should be a time when the subordinate can properly and respectfully discuss any differences. A good leader will be able to accommodate their unrest and listen to their concerns. It may be through the power of the Holy Spirit that the Lord will open the eyes of the leader to see from a different perspective and write the wrong if there be any! However, taking the dog by the tail and creating confusion in the camp is not the right way to handle any matter.

"And Samuel said, Hath the Lord as great delight in burnt offerings and sacrifices, as in obeying the voice of the Lord? Behold, to obey is better than sacrifice, and to hearken than the fat of rams."

1st Samuel 15:22

Obedience places you in a great position to be blessed. List below the blessings bestowed on those who obey, as written in Deuteronomy 28

Bishop Rosette Coney

#6 DON'T GET CAUGHT IN THE MOUTH TRAP!

"But as he which hath called you is holy, so be ye holy in all manner of conversation."
-    1Peter 1:15

The trap...

A trap is a snare that imprisons the subject; to restrain or fence in.   People often become prisoners of those who speak negatively about pastors and leaders. Believe me, many of you are not strong enough to override this powerful demonic spirit. Yes, it is a demonic spirit—a spirit of the flesh that leads to destruction. The LORD takes this kind of behavior very seriously (Numbers 12:1-10).

Godly fear seems to be something of the past— people today feel free to express negative thoughts about their pastors and church leaders in the open, not caring or minding the souls that would be adversely affected by this behavior.

If you become captivated by a pastor or leader basher, you will be as guilty as they are—you become an accomplice to the crime. It will be hard for you to escape from the clutches of this sin. It is not right; and remember that <u>all unrighteousness is sin</u>.

Don't you get caught up in this ghastly practice! It's a trap set by Satan, himself. This behavior is very contagious, and before you know it, you'll be repeating everything said to you, to somebody else —whether it is true, exaggerated, or false.

My sisters and brothers, watch how you address leadership with your mouth. It's not always what you say, but **how** you say it.

Watch your step, and don't get caught in the trap.

Ask God for wisdom and he'll show you how to detect the trap and give you the strength needed to jump over it.

"Death and life are in the power of the tongue: and they that love it shall eat the fruit thereof " *(Proverbs 18:21).*

What's going on with that tongue?...

An exalted individual will often demonstrate the lack of respect and self-control with their tongue. Therefore, when it comes to speaking, they will not honor or esteem their peers or anyone over them. <u>The Bible says in Proverbs 16:18 "Pride *goeth* before destruction, and an haughty spirit before a fall</u>." (*"Humble yourselves therefore under the mighty hand of God, that he may exalt you in due time:" -- 1ˢᵗ Peter 5:6*)

When speaking, a demonstration of respect for others, especially those who are over you in the Lord, is something <u>practiced</u>. Practice makes permanent. *Honor all men, Love the brotherhood. Fear God. Honor the king (1ˢᵗ Peter 2:17).*

AFTER THOUGHT

If caught in the Mouth Trap, you could be destroyed...

When used improperly, your mouth could get you into a lot of trouble. The Word of God clearly indicates in Proverbs 18:21, *"Death and life are in the power of the tongue: and they that love it shall eat the fruit thereof."* You can put your feet on the seat and in your mouth at the same time, thus walking yourself into a valley of death.

The devil is real good at his game of catching good honest Christians in his mouth traps. He lures them into dangerous conversations that lead to a dark path of trouble. He knows those who are disgruntled about decisions made by leaders and gets them to voice their opinion to other weak Christians. He also points out other little nit-picking circumstances that birth bad feelings: situations like, being passed over for a position, not given the opportunity to sing or preach or praise dance, being called out for any misunderstandings between others in the group, and the list goes on. Once a person falls into the mouth trap, it's hard to climb out.

> *36 But I say unto you, That every idle word that men shall speak, they shall give account thereof in the day of judgment.37 For by thy words thou shalt be justified, and by thy words thou shalt be condemned.*
>
> Matthew 12:36-37

We truly have full control of what we say and what we do – "the devil made me do it" is a statement truly played out!   We have to take ownership of our mistakes in life. But I am wondering, "What measures can you take to avoid falling into the **mouth trap**?"

| |
| |
| |
| |
| |

Bishop Rosette Coney

#7 DON'T KILL THE SHEPHERD!

"Touch not mine anointed, and do my prophets
no harm."
-1st Chronicles 16:22

Understanding What a Shepherd is...

A shepherd is simply someone who looks after the sheep. They tend the herd, feed the flock, keeps them clean and protects them from all harm.

Generally speaking and from a spiritual aspect, the shepherd is the pastor of a church, and responsible for the welfare of the congregation.

I share here with you the various forms of shepherding:

- A pastor is a shepherd to the church.

- An elder or deacon is a shepherd within the body.
- A husband is a shepherd to his wife.
- Parents are shepherds to their children.
- A teacher is a shepherd to his students.
- An employer is a shepherd to his employees.
- An older child is a shepherd to his/her younger brothers and sisters.
- Anyone who in anyway leads anyone is a shepherd responsible for the care of another.

The Important Role of the Shepherd...

If you refer to Psalm 23, you can get a pretty good idea about the role of a shepherd.

- **A shepherd gives the sheep a sense of belonging:** He lets the sheep know that they are his, and they are trained not to follow strange voices. Notice John 10:4-5 - *"4 And when he putteth forth his own sheep, he goeth before them, and the sheep follow him: for they know his voice. 5 And a stranger will they not follow, but will flee from him: for they know not the voice of strangers.*

- **A shepherd knows the sheep in his care, and he knows them by name**: Notice John 10:14, *"I am the good shepherd, and know my sheep, and am known of mine"* Also notice John 10:3, *"To him the porter openeth; and the sheep hear his voice: and he calleth his own sheep by name, and leadeth them out"*.

- **A shepherd feeds the sheep:** Notice John 21:15-17, *"So when they had dined, Jesus saith to Simon Peter, Simon, son of Jonas, lovest thou me more than these? He saith unto him, Yea, Lord; thou knowest that I love thee. He saith unto him, Feed my lambs. He saith to him again the second time, Simon, son of Jonas, lovest thou me? He saith unto him, Yea, Lord; thou knowest that I love thee. He saith unto him, Feed my sheep. He saith unto him the third time, Simon, son of Jonas, lovest thou me? Peter was grieved because he said unto him the third time, Lovest thou me? And he said unto him, Lord, thou knowest all things; thou knowest that I love thee. Jesus saith unto him, Feed my sheep"*

- **A shepherd makes sure the sheep are comfortable and at peace**: They also make sure the sheep does not feel pressured in any way. Notice Isaiah 40:11 – *"He shall feed his flock like a shepherd: he shall gather the lambs with his arm, and carry them in his bosom, and shall gently lead those that are with young."* Yes, the shepherd makes sure there is no lack with the sheep. Also, notice Jeremiah 23:4 - *"And I will set up shepherds over them which shall feed them: and they shall fear no more, nor be dismayed, neither shall they be lacking, saith the LORD."*

- **A shepherd leads – not drives - the sheep to a place where their thirst can be quenched:** If the sheep trusts the voice of the shepherd, they will follow the shepherd to that safe place of refreshing. Notice 1st Peter 5:1-4, *"The elders which are among you I exhort, who am also an elder, and a witness of the sufferings of Christ, and also a partaker of the glory that shall be revealed: Feed the* *flock of God which is among you, taking the oversight thereof, not by constraint, but willingly; not for filthy lucre, but of a ready mind; Neither as being lords over God's heritage, but being ensamples to the flock. And when the chief Shepherd shall appear, ye shall receive a crown of glory that fadeth not away"*

- **God assigns the role and position of a shepherd**: And because of that, the shepherd should not do it out of compulsion, but voluntarily. It should not be done for money, but willingly. The individual given this role, as shepherd, should not be lords over the sheep, but lead them being examples to the flock. The result is that they will receive a crown of glory.

- **The shepherd leads by still waters.** The sheep will drown in fast moving water. Their wool is like a sponge that absorbs the water so that the sheep cannot swim out. The shepherd again leads them to the still waters that they can drink without being afraid of drowning.

- **The shepherd restores the soul of the sheep.** The soul is the mind, will, and emotions of the sheep. The shepherd does this by <u>affirming</u> the sheep, rather than being critical of everything they do. The shepherd encourages the sheep, rather than discouraging them.

  a. He **affirms** the sheep rather than bring critical.

  b. He **encourages** the sheep rather than being discouraging to them.

  c. He **instructs** rather than condemning them.

  d. He **speaks blessing** over them rather than cursing them.

  e. He **protects** them rather than feeding them to the wolves.

  f. He **gathers them together** with the flock rather than scattering them in the wilderness.

- **The shepherds bring healing.** In Ezekiel 34:4, God rebukes the shepherds of Israel for not strengthening the flock. *"The diseased have ye not strengthened, neither have ye healed that which was sick, neither have ye bound up that which was broken, neither have ye brought again that which was driven away, neither have ye sought that which was lost; but with force and with cruelty have ye ruled them"*. And in the New Testament, Jesus sent out His twelve disciples to heal the lost sheep of Israel. He told them, in Matthew 10:7-8, *"And as ye go, <u>preach</u>, saying, The kingdom of heaven is at hand. <u>Heal</u> the sick, <u>cleanse</u> the lepers, <u>raise</u> the dead, <u>cast out</u> devils: <u>freely ye have received, freely give.</u>"*

- **The shepherds lead the sheep into righteousness**. He leads the sheep by being a good example before them. This method shows them how to walk in the right paths. The sheep can sometimes become childlike, and the Word of God instructs leaders to train them up in the way that they should go (Proverbs 22:6).

- **The shepherd is also willing to go after the lost sheep**. Luke15:3-7 relays the story of how the shepherd was so concerned about the whereabouts of the lost sheep that he went after that sheep and searched until it was found. He was willing to leave the flock in pursuit of that one that was lost. *"And he spake this parable unto them, saying, What man of you, having an hundred sheep, if he lose one of them, doth not leave the ninety and nine in the wilderness, and go after that which is lost, until he find it? And when he hath found it, he layeth it on his shoulders, rejoicing. And when he cometh home, he calleth together his friends and neighbours, saying unto them, Rejoice with me; for I have found my sheep which was lost. I say unto you, that likewise joy shall be in heaven over one sinner that repenteth, more than over ninety and nine just persons, which need no repentance"*.   I've heard it said that the shepherd breaks the legs of the wondering sheep so that it does not stray off again. To me, this denotes a sense of dependency on the shepherd's part, he wants the sheep to depend on him to meet all of their needs. Also, loving discipline requires restrictions to be placed on the sheep for their own safety. A shepherd that truly loves the sheep will chasten that sheep for its own good.

- **The shepherd makes sure the sheep is secured and safe**. Even if the sheep have to walk through the valley of the shadow of death, confidence can be their guide because the shepherd is there to comfort them. A good shepherd is willing to give up his life for the sheep. John 10:11 share an example of how Jesus feels about His sheep as a good shepherd, *"I am the good shepherd: the good shepherd giveth his life for the sheep."* A good shepherd will never leave his sheep for the wolves to attack and carry off to completely devour them. The shepherd uses his rod (authority) and his staff (to pull the sheep safely out of the pit of trouble).

- **A good shepherd does his job because of the love for his sheep**; not for a measly pay check. Notice John 10:12-13 - *"But he that is an hireling, and not the shepherd, whose own the sheep are not, seeth the wolf coming, and leaveth the sheep, and fleeth: and the wolf catcheth them, and scattereth the sheep. The hireling fleeth, because he is an hireling, and careth not for the sheep"*.

- **The shepherd is willing to fight for the sheep**. Look at David (the shepherd) in the story of how he was willing to present himself before King Saul as a candidate to fight the giant, Goliath. Notice 1 Samuel 17:32-36 - *"And David said to Saul, Let no man's heart fail because of him; thy servant will go and fight with this Philistine. And Saul said to David, Thou art not able to go against this Philistine to fight with him: for thou art but a youth, and he a man of war from his* *youth. And David said unto Saul, Thy servant kept his father's sheep, and there came a lion, and a bear, and took a lamb out of the flock: And I went out after him, and smote him, and delivered it out of his mouth: and when he arose against me, I caught him by his beard, and smote him, and slew him. Thy servant slew both the lion and the bear: and this uncircumcised Philistine shall be as one of them, seeing he hath defied the armies of the living God".* David went after the enemy full forced and won the victory.

- The shepherd prepares the sheep for display, right before witnesses. The shepherd spends time making sure the sheep are presentable before men. They spare nothing to make the sheep look good – if the shepherd takes good care of the sheep, they will be healthy and strong and able to multiply. Now, the enemy will, of course, be watching the sheep, but, the good shepherd will be watching also, with eagle eyes.

- The shepherd anoints the sheep with oil – to overflow. The oil represents a sense of worth. The shepherd appreciates the sheep enough to recognize their worthiness. They take special precautions to spot if any of the sheep are ill. They anoint them with oil. Notice James 5:14, *"Is any sick among you? let him call for the elders of the church; and let them pray over him, anointing him with oil in the name of the Lord"*

- **The shepherd watches out for and prays for the sheep**. The shepherd places a hedge around the sheep to protect them from outside danger through prayer. He binds the enemy to protect the sheep, and recognizes a wolf that may be dressed in sheep's clothing. Notice Matthew 7:15 – "Beware of false prophets, which come to you in sheep's clothing, but inwardly they are ravening wolves."

- **The shepherd causes the sheep cup to run over**. The good shepherd is not stingy towards the sheep, but blesses the sheep beyond measure. The shepherd blesses the sheep through <u>giving attention</u> (giving quality time to), <u>praise</u>, <u>affirmation</u>, <u>thanksgiving</u>, <u>provision</u>, and <u>promotion</u>. He also rejoices with the sheep when they make progress.

- **The sheep should see the shepherd as one of goodness and mercy**. The shepherd should carry themselves in a manner that makes the sheep feel good about singing their praises. The sheep should not be fearful of the shepherd – the one who protects them. This will cause the sheep to want to stay and graze around the shepherd. If they sheep stray away, they will be in a hurry to return home when they think pleasant thoughts of the shepherd. Notice Psalm 23:6 – *"Surely goodness and mercy shall follow me all the days of my life: and I will dwell in the house of the LORD for ever."*

If you plot to kill the shepherd, the flock will be destroyed. You may not always like or agree with your shepherd or leader, but you've got to have enough trust and faith in God to handle situations that arise from disagreements.

In addition, if you kill the shepherd, the flock will scatter and be eaten by the wolves. Notice Ezekiel 34:5-6... *"And they were scattered, because there is no shepherd: and they became meat to all the beasts of the field, when they were scattered. My sheep wandered through all the mountains, and upon every high hill: yea, my flock was scattered upon all the face of the earth, and none did search or seek after them."*

How can you kill the shepherd? You kill the shepherd with your mouth—your rumors and assumptions. You kill them by coming up against them and causing unrest among the other members. Don't do that! For God's sake, let the shepherd live!

> "And when I passed by thee, and saw thee polluted in thine own blood, I said unto thee when thou wast in thy blood, Live; yea, I said unto thee when thou wast in thy blood, Live."
>
> Ezekiel 16:6

AFTER THOUGHT

Let's do all we can to keep the shepherd alive and well...

As much as the shepherd needs the sheep to lead, the sheep needs the shepherd to lead them. Who wants a shepherd who is all broke down, stressed out, detached from reality and their responsibilities, to lead them? No one! Just as shepherds have their own responsibilities, the sheep of the fold has a charge as well.

The Lord leads the shepherd who leads the sheep. Because the sheep in most cases cannot navigate their own way, the shepherd is there to guide them and lead them into green pastures. The sheep need restoring from time to time – they need to be pulled out of the valley and the shadows of death; they need to be comforted and cared for. For a successful correlation between them, both shepherd and sheep have to work together in the spirit of unity, respect and love.

All sheep need to determine within themselves that they are going to do all they can to help keep the shepherd alive and well. This involves obedience, love, dedication, support (financially and spiritually through prayer), it is equally important to lend a helping hand; both physically, and also emotionally (sometimes the shepherd may need a shoulder to cry on).

"10 Be kindly affectioned one to another with brotherly love; in honour preferring one another; 11 Not slothful in business; fervent in spirit; serving the Lord; 12 Rejoicing in hope; patient in tribulation; continuing instant in prayer; 13 Distributing to the necessity of saints; given to hospitality. 14 Bless them which persecute you: bless, and curse not. 15 Rejoice with them that do rejoice, and weep with them that weep."

Romans 12:10-15

So, now that you know what it will take to keep your shepherd alive, what do you plan to do to assist them in the following areas of need?

Obedience	
Love	
Dedication	
Support	
Physical	
Emotional	

Bishop Rosette Coney

#8 GIVING HONOR TO THE SEAT

"Render therefore to all their dues: tribute to whom tribute is due;
custom to whom custom; fear to whom fear; honor to whom honor."
-Romans 13:7

What is meant by honor...

Honor is respect, admiration, esteem, regard, reference, devotion.

Honoring the seat ..

You have the obligation of honoring the seat (position) where your leader sits, even if you are at odds with them.

Today, that seems to be a major problem with folks. Jesus said, "A prophet is not without honor, but in his own country, and among his own kin, and in his own house. (Mark 6:4)

Let's face it! There are no perfect leaders. The greatest leader in the world has flaws. Everybody has them—yet, the flaws help to make them who they are—they are genuine. When you purchase an expensive item made of a good grain of leather, the flaws in that leather represent its authenticity. There is no dishonorable piece of leather. It is what it is. Well, it's the same way with your leader. For God's sake, let them be who they are. Honor them for what they represent. Honor them for their works' sake. Honor them because **God** told us to honor them.

The Word can speak for itself...

In God's Word, there are many supporting scriptures hinging on the importance of leadership. To name a few:

Philippians 2:3 – *"Let nothing be done through*

strife or vainglory; but in lowliness of mind let each esteem the other better than themselves."

Matthew 20:25-28 - *"But Jesus called them unto him, and said, Ye know that the princes of the Gentiles exercise dominion over them, and they that are great exercise authority upon them. But it shall not be so among you: but whosoever will be great among you, let him be your minister; And whosoever will be chief among you, let him be your servant: Even as the Son of man came not to be ministered unto, but to minister, and to give his life a ransom for many."*

1 Timothy 5:17-18 - *"Let the elders that rule well be counted worthy of double honour, especially they who labour in the word and doctrine. [18]For the scripture saith, Thou shalt not muzzle the ox that treadeth out the corn. And, The labourer is worthy of his reward."*

1 Timothy 6:1 - *"Let as many servants as are under the yoke count their own masters worthy of all honour, that the name of God and his doctrine be not blasphemed."*

1 Peter 2:17-20 - *"Honour all men. Love the brotherhood. Fear God. Honor the king. Servants, be subject to your masters with all fear; not only to the good and gentle, but also to the froward. For this is thankworthy, if a man for conscience toward God endure grief, suffering wrongfully. For what glory is it, if, when ye be buffeted for your faults, ye shall take it patiently? but if, when ye do well, and suffer for it, ye take it patiently, this is acceptable with God."*

Demonstrating love and honor with a gift...

Finally, I share with you a principle that I've adopted a long time ago; the concept of never appearing before a leader empty – especially a leader assigned by God. In my spirit, I feel like the highest leader of the organization really represents God, so I never appear before them without a gift – I take that seriously. The thought, not the gift or the value thereof, matters. I share with you a few passages that support my idealism. Exodus 23:15 – "Thou shalt keep the feast of unleavened bread: (thou shalt eat unleavened bread seven days, as I commanded thee, in the time appointed of the month Abib; for in it thou camest out from Egypt: and none shall appear before me empty:)" and also Deuteronomy 16:16 *"Three times in a year shall all thy males appear before the Lord thy God in the place which he shall choose; in the feast of unleavened bread, and in the feast of weeks, and in the feast of tabernacles: and they shall not appear before the Lord empty:"*

AFTER THOUGHT

The Seat actually deserves the honor...

When giving honor to the seat, you are only giving that which is due. When there is an authority figure operating in the office of a leader, they are the governing power to be reckoned with. With this authority comes heavy responsibility for those they preside over – however high their position is, they must still report to someone even higher and with that responsibility comes accountability.

So with that in mind, the seat occupied by a leader must be respected at all times in order for any organization to run smoothly. The organizational chart must line up properly in more areas than just on paper. All leaders in their respective places should be honored, even if they are in charge of the clean-up department. Whatever practice you choose to use, your leader should not have to guess whether or not you honor them.

Take time to think about ways you can honor the seat,

even if you are at odds with the occupant of the seat:

Bishop Rosette Coney

#9 MISERY LOVES COMPANY

"For where envying and strife is, there is confusion and every evil work."
- James 3:16

Have you ever noticed that when someone is angry or upset with their leader, they try earnestly to pass their ill feelings on to others? This poisonous snake has destroyed many congregations and ministries.

The Bible speaks of Diotrephes in III John, who constantly caused discord among the people. His deeds included prating against leadership with malicious words, and not being willing to help the leaders succeed. Anyone who does good is of God, but anyone who does evil has not even seen God (*verse 11*). If you get wind of anyone who falls into this category—move yourself far from them. Notice 2nd Thessalonians 3:6 which reads, *"Now we command you, brethren, in the name of our Lord Jesus Christ, that ye withdraw yourselves from every brother that walketh disorderly, and not after the tradition which he received of us."*

Make it a practice to hang around spiritually strong people who love the Lord and honors leadership. Being around these types of people produces a pleasant atmosphere of peace. These are usually people who are busy doing the Master's business. They are supporters and not extortionists.

Those who stir up strife about leadership can be classified as evil seeds planted in the soil of unrighteousness. They are unhappy with themselves; and focus on the failure of others, while trying to mask their own bloopers. They leave a trail of complaints where ever they trod, and they seek to gain followers to spawn their own popularity.

These people slither into the hearts of potentially good people, and quickly corrupt their thinking. Before you know it, a conglomerate of dissatisfied, miserable, leader-haters are formed and they stunt the growth of any potentially successful organization or church.

Again, separate yourself from any such groupings, and remain focused. Stay on the path of purpose and you will win the prize of reaching your destiny.

AFTER THOUGHT

I'm miserable, and I want you to be miserable too...

That's what happens when you see or hear a person murmuring and complaining all the time about their leader. These individuals truly need a healing – from the inside out. Now, if you're not careful and prayerful, you can become one of those people. Sometimes you're not strong enough to convert them, and you may be caught up into their flavor and end up acting strangely towards your leader.

I would advise you to run in the opposite direction when you encounter one of these. They mean you no good, and will stop at nothing to have company in their play pen. The wrath of God comes upon the children of disobedience. A miserable leader-bashing person loves company.

Micah 7:1-7 puts it all in perspective...

"Woe is me! for I am as when they have gathered the summer fruits, as the grape gleanings of the vintage:

there is no cluster to eat: my soul desired the firstripe fruit. The good man is perished out of the earth: and there is none upright among men: they all lie in wait for blood; they hunt every man his brother with a net. That they may do evil with both hands earnestly, the prince asketh, and the judge asketh for a reward; and the great man, he uttereth his mischievous desire: so they wrap it up. The best of them is as a brier: the most upright is sharper than a thorn hedge: the day of thy watchmen and thy visitation cometh; now shall be their perplexity. Trust ye not in a friend, put ye not confidence in a guide: keep the doors of thy mouth from her that lieth in thy bosom. For the son dishonoureth the father, the daughter riseth up against her mother, the daughter in law against her mother in law; a man's enemies are the men of his own house. Therefore I will look unto the LORD; I will wait for the God of my salvation: my God will hear me."

What could you say to a miserable person to take the wind out of their sail?

#10 LEADERS GO THROUGH TOO

"Take, my brethren, the prophets, who have spoken in the name of the Lord,
for an example of suffering affliction, and of patience."
-James 5:10

People of all levels go through a great deal in coping with day to day obstacles and challenges. But, leaders go through a lot too. Their load is much heavier than those they lead. Let's look at some of the challenges that **LEADERS** in particular have to face:

L - Loneliness

We've heard from time to time that familiar quote: "It's lonely at the top". It's difficult to trust people in general. So often, leaders are left with no one to bleed out to. People are intimidated by their titles and positions and therefore tend to shy away from them. Leaders have no one to share their problems, their fears, pains and or weaknesses.

E - Emptiness

Pastors especially, give out much and wait to hear from the Lord. Many times the answers never seems to come and a great feeling of emptiness overshadows them. They sometimes feel like God has forgotten them. They are far removed from the passage of scripture in Matthew 28:20 "...and, lo, I am with you always, even unto the end of the world. Amen." The leading prophets of old experienced this feeling.

A - Abused

Believe it or not, leaders experience various forms of abuse from time to time. They are disrespected by individuals who misunderstand them and those who just don't care for any form of leadership over them (these are often referred to as rebels). They have struggles with family issues - when family members are jealous of the time they spend doing their jobs. This adds pressure to their already pressure-filled role. Moses in the Bible was bombarded with complaints from those he led out of Egypt. Exodus gives a clear picture of the abuse suffered by Moses as he led the children of Israel to the promise land.

D - Defeated

When leaders give their very best, and sometimes it seems like their best just isn't good enough, they feel defeated. When they struggle with people who they are trying to develop and grow by depositing good seeds of knowledge into them, and they can't seem to get it together, the leader feels defeated. When a pastor works hard at growing their church and there are no new members to measure their sense of growth, they feel like a failure, and need much encouragement.

E - Exhausted

A tired leader is often not able to put their best foot forward. Suffering from exhaustion hinders the performance of any good leader. A burned out leader becomes unhealthy - mentally and physically and is of no good to themselves or anyone else. This happened to Moses and he became very frustrated. Sometime a leader cuts their slices too thin - they take on too many people problems and time consuming projects.

R - Restless

When a leader curls up in bed with all of their problems and everyone else's, there is no room in the bed for rest and sleep. Rest and sleep leaves to go to visit someone else. A leader cannot properly function in a restless condition - they become irritable, depressed, short-tempered and hard to get along with. Eight hours of sleep are required to rebuild and replace vital body cells. Leaders really need their rest because it takes a boat load of energy to lead, guide, direct, encourage, correct, and teach people.

S -Stress

The final blow to leaders is stress. There are so many hanging up their mallets because the stress that comes with leadership is too much to handle. The pressure of leading people, whether in the business world, the home, or on the spiritual circuit can at times be too great. Stress affects every area of a human being, and can sometimes cause irreparable damage. There are many biblical scriptures designed to keep leaders from turning into a stress ball and bouncing into the world of insanity. One of those is the familiar passage that says... "Casting all your care upon him; for he careth for you." - 1 Peter 5:7

When you put this all together, you see how important it is to take your feet off the seat of those who lead – they have enough to go through, without being walked all over. Cherish the leader, love them and do all you can to support them in their efforts. Try to understand them and not change them. God is the only one who has a license to change your leader if they are traveling down the wrong path. Step back and let Him do His job. Trust Him and let Him show you what He is capable of doing. This takes patience on your part and in some cases, it takes tolerance and endurance. The end results will be one of success and not failure – when God has His way.

> *Be that support for your leader that lifts he or she to reach their greatest potential.*

AFTER THOUGHT

I understand now what my leader goes through...

Seeking to understand what your leader goes through allows you to walk a mile in their shoes. Once you truly understand their battles, you can see how important it is to keep your feet off the seat.

Leaders sometime suffer in silence – they try to protect the sheep from worrying about them. Strong leaders try not to bleed before the people. They mask their hurt and pain and cover up any signs of weakness.

Each individual should take to heart the welfare of their leader and do all in their power to make their job a little more bearable. Becoming a part of the solution and not a part of the problem should be the goal of every person who values the success of their organization or church. A good foundation contributes greatly to the building up of a strong house.

Remember these leaders – don't forget about them – help lighten their load, and truly consider the hardship they go through.

> *"Remember them which have the rule over you, who have spoken unto you the word of God: whose faith follow, considering the end of their conversation."*
>
> *Hebrews 13:7*

What can you do to help lighten the load of your leader?

#11 REMEMBER... YOU GET BACK WHAT YOU GIVE

Now, if you walk all over your pastor or leader, somebody's gonna walk all over you. That's right! You get back what you give. Galatians 6:7 reads, *"Be not deceived; God is not mocked: for whatsoever a man soweth, that shall he also reap."*

Don't worry if you are being treated unfairly by someone in authority who presides over you. Give God credit for being an all knowing and all powerful God. He'll take care of the situation for you. **You must be patient** and do all that you are supposed to do. Proverbs 20:22 reads, *"Say not thou, I will recompense evil; but wait on the LORD, and he shall save thee."*

Let me share with you some scripture on having patience:

Psalms 37:7 - *"Rest in the Lord, and wait patiently for him: fret not thyself because of him who prospereth in his way, because of the man who bringeth wicked devices to pass."* In other words, just quiet down before GOD, remain prayerful in rough situations. Don't worry yourself about those who climb the ladder of success, elbowing their way up to the top. Their day is coming!

Psalms 40:1 – *"I waited patiently for the LORD; and he inclined unto me, and heard my cry."* God's ears are not dull to your cries of unfair treatment. He has the day circled on His calendar of when He plans to avenge you. Just wait patiently for Him – He's coming to your rescue.

Ecclesiastes 7:8 – *"Better is the end of a thing than the beginning thereof: and the patient in spirit is better than the proud in spirit."* How you end up is much better than how you start. If you remain humble, patient, steadfast, and steady in respecting your leaders, you will certainly end up on top.

Romans 12:12 – *"Rejoicing in hope; patient in tribulation; continuing instant in prayer;"* It's not what you go through – it's how you go through it. When experiencing unfair treatment by a leader, learn to say "hallelujah anyhow", remain prayerful and look forward with a hopeful spirit to the day when it all will end. Put on a happy face until then!

And please don't forget what Romans 12:19 says, *"Dearly beloved, avenge not yourselves, but rather give place unto wrath: for it is written, Vengeance is mine; I will repay, saith the Lord."* Don't fight back; try to discover beauty in your leader. If you have it in you, try hard to get along with them. Don't insist on getting even; that's really not for you to do. God is the One who will determine the penalty for wrong doing.

Listen, be kind, loving and respectful, it's going to come back to you.

AFTER THOUGHT

If you don't want it to come back on you, don't give it out...

Doing things in the flesh will cause you to reap things in the flesh – doing things in the spirit will cause you to reap spiritual, damage-proof, everlasting, blessings. There is no good thing within the flesh – so says the Word of God. Romans 7:18 reads, *"For I know that in me (that is, in my flesh,) dwelleth no good thing: for to will is present with me; but how to perform that which is good I find not."* To this end, it is not advisable to execute revenge or outrageous behavior upon anyone. It always finds its way back to you. Yes, you will reap what you sow. Sowing good seeds, even when bad weeds are thrown your way will produce for you a far greater reward.

Remember that as someone is over you, you are also over some type of function in your life – it may be that you are a parent or an older sibling. What you dish out will be served right back at you.

"*Be not deceived; God is not mocked:*

for whatsoever a man soweth,

that shall he also reap."

Galatians 6:7

Think about whose life you need to sow a good seed into right now - write it down to commit yourself to carrying it out?

Bishop Rosette Coney

#12 APPRECIATING A LEADER WHO'S ON FIRE

"...Who maketh his angels spirits, and his ministers a flame of fire." - Hebrews 1:7b

Serving Under a Leader Who's on **Fire**

_F_ervent (eager)

_I_ nspiring (motivating)

_R_adical (progressive)

_E_ nthusiastic (passionate)

Let's first examine the word "Fire" – The World Book Dictionary defines it as "flame, heat and light caused by something burning". It is also defined as something <u>hot</u>, <u>brilliant</u> or <u>glowing</u>. Figuratively speaking, it is also considered the heat of a feeling; readiness to act; passion, fervor, enthusiasm or excitement.

There is a fire glowing inside of every good leader. We don't want to do anything that will put the fire out or cause it to get weak. Leaders, themselves, have the power and authority to decide how this fire inside of them will affect their own lives and leadership skills. But those who follow the leader have a cup of water with the capability of dousing that fire in them.

<u>A Leader on Fire is Ready to Act</u>– When there is a fire burning inside of your leader, they are earnestly ready and eager to get to work on God's behalf. They strive to do all they can for the kingdom of God, and it becomes their hope and physical quest in every waking moment of their lives. You can truly appreciate a leader like that! Philippians 1:20 reads, *"According to my earnest expectation and my hope, that in nothing I shall be ashamed, but that with all boldness, as always, so now also Christ shall be magnified in my body, whether it be by life, or by* *death."*

A Leader With Passion – Fire brings out the passion in them. Leaders are passionate about everything in their charge, and they do all they can to make it work. The passion remains even through suffering and disappointments. Where there is passion, there is power!

A Leader With Fervor – Diligence, dedication and commitment are anchored to fervor. The fire inside of them drives them to be dedicated to any task assigned to their hands. Romans 12:8 incorporates the statement, *"...he that ruleth, with diligence;"*

A Leader With Enthusiasm or Excitement – The enthusiasm, excitement and the fire inside of a leader generates sparks, and will cause all who are around them to demonstrate that same vigor. Philemon 1:7 reads, *"For we have great joy and consolation in thy love, because the bowels of the saints are refreshed by thee, brother."*

Yes, within these types of leaders exist an eager, motivating, progressive and passionate spirit – waiting to be set free to fulfill the assigned mission.

You will want to serve under a leader with this spirit, because it will bring out the very best in you as well; you certainly will not want to walk all over their seat, your feet might get burned.

Do not be bound by intimidation from working under an enthusiastic leader. Instead, free your spirit by abolishing *doubt* and *fear*. Philippians 4:13 says, *"I can do all things through Christ which strengthens me."* Let the Fire within you move you to thrust forward into the path which God has personally designed for YOU. When a great leader inspires you to perform a task, remember that nobody can do your job like you can! Nobody can sing your song like you can! Nobody can communicate your thoughts like you can! Nobody can touch a soul like you can! Nobody is just like YOU. It takes different embers to keep each fire burning. Discover the embers that God has customized specifically for you when a leader that's on fire ignites you. The scents and aroma emitted from your combined efforts will be different than any other. Team work makes the dream work!

As a team, working with your leader, let your flames fly high – reach beyond your limit – let the fire burn within. Set your course of action on fire! Get busy! Get ready to become a trailblazer for the cause of righteousness as you serve under and support your enthusiastic leader!

AFTER THOUGHT

You can't afford to let that fire go out...

Serving under a boring, dull, non-motivating, slothful, uninspiring leader can cause you to become the same way ("Like priest like people").

You can be such a blessing to your organization if you become the log that keeps the fire burning. You can be the one who encourages, motivates and inspires your leader to be great. You can be the one strong table leg that holds the table top together. The other legs may have a loose screw here and there – but you can be the tight one that keeps the entire table from falling apart.

If you serve under a leader who is becoming tired and discouraged in their role, take the time to talk to your leader by the way side, and respectfully make suggestions that will help spark up that fire again in them. Yes, become that log.

> *"Let him that is taught in the word communicate unto him that teacheth in all good things."*
>
> *Galatians 6:6*

What can you say to your leader to turn the fire up in them?

Bishop Rosette Coney

#13 LEARNING TO ACCEPT A NEW LEADER

You may not know your new leader well enough to trust them immediately, but you should know ***God*** well enough to trust Him and the decisions He makes. Keep in mind that God is all Powerful and rules the whole world. Not one sparrow falls to the ground that He doesn't know about — not one strand of hair falls from your head that He can't account for. Yes, God knows that you just lost your 435th strand of hair for this year (Math 10:30).

When you decide to gracefully accept a new leader assigned over you, you are telling God, "Yes – I trust You!" When you trust God, your path in life will be smooth. The Lord tells us in Proverbs to trust Him with all of our hearts, He further encourages us not to lean to our own understanding, but to acknowledge Him in all of our ways. This will give Him leverage for directing our paths (Proverbs 3:5-6)

His decision of who leads us may not always be our first pick; but I don't believe He asks our opinion. He always knows what is best for us, and He certainly knows what He wants us to learn from serving under a leader of His choosing.

Whoever becomes our new leader, God is the One who will give the growth and increase in our lives, not the new leader. Remember the passage in 1st Corinthians 3:4-6:

For while one saith, I am of Paul; and another, I am of Apollos; are ye not carnal?

Who then is Paul, and who is Apollos, but ministers by whom ye believed, even as the Lord gave to every man?

I have planted, Apollos watered; but God gave the increase.

When Joshua took over after Moses' death, the people were very supportive. They loved Moses, but they knew that they needed leadership to cross over into Jordan, so they graciously accepted the new order of things. Even though Joshua was going through his own grief issues of losing Moses, the people obeyed willingly. They declared to Joshua, *"Whatever you have commanded us, we will do, and wherever you send us, we will go. Just as we fully obeyed Moses, so we will obey you. Only may the Lord your God be with you as He was with Moses. Whoever rebels against your word and does not obey your words, whatever you may command them, will be put to death. Only be strong and courageous!"* (Joshua 1:16-18) Can you do the same thing?

AFTER THOUGHT

Disband any preconceived thoughts about your new leader...

When a new leader is introduced to a congregation or establishment, the people usually form preconceived ideas about them. They form opinions on how they dress, what they say, how they look or where they came from. This is a normal reaction of the flesh.

Now, taking a look at the new leader from a spiritual viewpoint, you may begin to pray immediately for them ...

- pray that they will be sensitive to the needs of the people
- pray that they will take time to get to know the people individually
- pray that the people will receive them in the spirit of love
- pray that the people will do all they can to make them feel welcomed
- pray that they will not immediately introduce new policies and procedures

- pray that they will hear and respond to the voice of God
- pray that they will not become lords over God's people
- and the list goes on…

Everyone plays a role in helping to make the transition in the *changing of the guards* a pleasant one and not a tumultuous one.

.

> *"Obey them that have the rule over you, and submit yourselves: for they watch for your souls, as they that must give account, that they may do it with joy, and not with grief: for that is unprofitable for you."*
> *Hebrews 13:17*

What can you do to help make a new leader feel welcomed?

Bishop Rosette Coney

#14 NEVER FORGET THEM

"² And we beseech you, brethren, to know them which labour among you, and are over you in the Lord, and admonish you; ¹³ And to esteem them very highly in love for their work's sake. And be at peace among yourselves."

1 Thessalonians 5:12-13

How could I ever forget all the awesome giant leaders in my life who poured into my spirit, my mind and my soul the lessons learned in their lives and the experiences they encountered that helped to make them giants in my eyes.

My dearly beloved mother, the late Mrs. Louise Henderson, who was not only a dedicated deaconess of her church, but my coach, my friend and a perfect example of faithfulness. I am reaping today from the tithes she paid for me as a small child. I will never forget her. She was taken up into the arms of the Lord so swiftly that I never got a chance to say the final "thank you, Mommy." I'm so glad that I didn't put my feet all over her seat of leadership in my life.

My handsome father, the late Richard Henderson, whose voice and face I inherited. He was so musically gifted, and he deposited music into my soul – thanks, Daddy!

My grandfather, the late Reverend Henry C. Williams, such an impact he left on my life! His strength gave me strength, his biblical knowledge gave me inspiration to draw my first illustrations of the stories in Bible. The loving teamwork he and my grandmother, the late Mrs. Daisy Williams, orchestrated with their relationship with their ten children demonstrated powerful management skills. I will never forget them.

All of my aunts and uncles, who swarmed around my sisters and I as we grew up and developed into adult women. We had the surround sound of love, organization, order, and structure on a foundation of godliness. What perfect examples they were for us. And my Aunt Lee – what can I say about her? Even with being born in 1914, her mind and stamina is just as strong today as it was 50 years ago. She is my mother, my aunt, my inspiration, my example, my anchor and my greatest critic. I will never forget her!

In the corporate world, I had great leaders as well who inspired me and corrected me when I needed it. Jon Thomas, Vice President of HR inspired me to learn a new word every day – that really built up and strengthened my vocabulary. I will never forget it!

The spiritual giants in my life, well, I'll never forget them either. Although some of them are sleeping in the heart of the earth, these people deposited into my life seeds of wisdom and grace that acted as a springboard to catapult me into who I am today.

The **late Bishop M. L. Jewell** taught me discipline in following leadership. She taught it over and over again – in and out of season – leadership training was coming out of my ears! The **late Bishop Ninious Randall** stood tall as a shining example of how to act when you know your identity. He taught us to always think for ourselves and not follow the crowd. He wanted us to be proactive and not reactive. I will never forget them!

What can I say about the great leader, the **late Dr. Naomi Manning**, my Bishop, my Friend, my inspiration. She showed me how to work hard and still enjoy life abundantly. She had such class and dignity. She never failed to show her appreciation for the person who felt the least of all; always a thank you card; always a birthday card: and always a thinking of you card. She never forgot to say "Thank You". I gleaned from her knowledge and her professionalism. Dr. Manning was a professional singer and songwriter, and some of her songs are still ringing in my heart today. I will never forget her for that!

The **late Bishop Elleree Coney** was not only my mother in-law, but also my motivator, and she cheered me on – gently pushing me into my destiny. The words of encouragement she planted in my ears sustained me during trying times. I will never forget her! **Bishop Gerald Brown** taught me how to keep my mind on my mission and my mission on my mind, and **Bishop Marva Neal** was a strong shoulder to cry on. I will never forget these two for that!

From **Bishop Faye Moore**, I received the knowledge of how to be more compassionate to those who just don't know how to get it right. I also learned how to read it for myself and not take for granted statements presumed to be in the Bible. I won't forget her!

Bishop Millicent Hunter made sure that I knew it was ok to be classy, chic, cool and clever at the same time. She schooled me on the ins and outs of being a female bishop and pastor, but still a submissive and loving wife, who is also sensitive to the needs of her husband. It feels good having him sit by my side in the pulpit. I won't forget her!

Bishop Anthony Harley made me realize that I am truly a leader, personally created by the hands of God, and there's nothing I can do about it. I will never forget him for that!

What can I say about the wisdom and humility of my spiritual father, **Dr. Eric A. Lambert, II**, Presiding Bishop of the Bethel Deliverance International Fellowship of Churches? I am forever a student, learning how to slow down and be in the uninterrupted presence of the Almighty God. His leadership techniques when implemented produces success every time. I am awed by you, Bishop. I will never forget you nor any of these other giants in my life!

A PRAYER OF REPENTANCE

Most gracious God, and Father of all, I come to You in humble submission. Please search my heart, my soul, my mind and my spirit today. If You find anything unpleasing to You, please take it out and create in me a clean heart and renew the right spirit within me.

your standards. Please forgive me if at any time I have rejected, offended, or dishonored anyone you have placed over me in the Lord, to watch for my soul. Teach me how to love with a pure heart and transform my mind, so that I can learn to think positive thoughts and accept what you, oh God, allow to take place in my life.

Thank You for Your forgiveness! I feel your unfailing love, abiding peace and your presence in my heart today.

Mold me and make me what you would have me to be. My desire is to please you in all things.

Accept me, Lord, and use me as a vessel to help encourage and strengthen others spiritually. In Jesus' name I pray. Amen!

Encouraging Words From The Author

I DISCOVERED WHO I WAS...

In the various leadership roles that I was ushered into, I experienced disappointments, but never defeat. I was at the point many times of giving up, but never did I retreat. I experienced misunderstandings, but they didn't make me quit or give up; they actually catapulted me into a zone where I was able to discover who I really was. I was Rosette – the artist – the musical composer – the wife – the mother – the sister - the friend – the motivator – the leader - and most important, the servant.

I served like I knew who I was, and I served like I knew Who sent me to serve – which isn't always an easy thing to do. The thing that made it challenging is the fact that some people didn't get the email from

God validating me as the aggressive server. I served my leaders from the low end – running to get the female leaders slippers to change into from their dress shoes; making sure they had something to eat or drink; sending greeting cards to others that I made myself and signed their names to; sending them encouraging letters and cards when I felt they were having a bad day; having handy wipes available if something got on their clothing, and making sure that their children were well taken care of emotionally and physically. Although these leaders are now sleeping in the heart of the earth, none of them could ever say that I put my feet on their seats. I respected them, I loved them and I honored them – simply because I knew who I was and my purpose.

Oh, the names I was called for serving with the spirit of excellence, both in the spiritual arena and the business world. Names like butt-kisser, flunky, phony, fool-for-favors, and a show-off, to name a few, is what I was called. Now, listen to this, I was even called names for faithfully serving my husband with love. Is that crazy, or what?

One thing that I want the readers to know is the fact

that the misunderstandings, the ridicules and teasing did not feel good at all – these things hurt, especially when they come from those who said they loved you. But the trick to overcoming such tantalizing experiences is to be grounded in the Word of God. The Word never lied. When you read the NIV version of Psalm 109 and see the prayer David prayed against those who gave him a hard time, you see where he must have felt some relief in what he hoped God would do to those who came up against him. I never wished evil against my aggressors, but I prayed that God would keep me in control so that I would not act out in the flesh, and that I would trust Him to be my Avenger. I can truly say that He kept me in the midst of it all. With God on my side, I am successfully leading my medium sized church with a mega church mentality – and that's because I know who I am!

Bishop Rosette Coney

MY ACCEPTANCE OF THE CALL TO LEAD...

I would like to share with you a few experiences of how I accepted the truth, that a leader was being birthed within me before receiving any titles.

My sisters and I have been singing together as a group since we were in elementary school. Although I was the middle child, giving orders to my siblings was natural for me: what we were going to sing; what we were going to wear. Amazingly they were humble enough to accept my suggestions without a fight. As we got older, I even purchased for them the outfits we were to wear – pretty bold, I think.

At my local church, I was always starting something, and what I started somehow benefited the church through the assignments and appointments I received: president of the usher board, choir directress, social club, founder and president of the women's outreach ministry ("WOM") – where we reached out to so many needy souls with extended helping hands, president of the pastor's aide committee, youth pastor, editor and writer of the national church newsletter, national praise team, ghost writer for the senior bishop of the national church, and various capacities too numerous to mention. In my large upper tier family (my mother was the youngest of ten), I was also able to recognize my leadership skills when I was elected as chairman of the Williams/Walker Family Reunion – what an honor! But even in a loving family structure, I faced oppositions and challenges.

I can remember being such a young girl, conducting the tri state mass choir at my church, and was way too little to be seen, so they built me a portable platform to stand on and carry around when the choir sang at different locations. I directed that choir with everything in me – I had a passion for it. Passion will take you places you never thought you would be.

In the workforce, my leadership skills were recognized as well, sometimes with much opposition because of my age. There were good times, and there were also bad times. Dealing with people of all ages, ethnic groups, experiences and views could be quite challenging at times. But because I always kept a good sense of humor and was a people lover, I never took the challenges seriously. The challenges actually strengthened me for the destiny God had chiseled out for my life. I laughed a lot and brought laughter into the lives of everyone around me. The gift of laughter kept me from crying when I was being attacked by haters while operating in any of these leadership roles.

Bishop Rosette Coney

ABOUT THE AUTHOR

Bishop Rosette Coney was born the middle child to the late Richard and Louise Henderson, in the City of Philadelphia, PA and is inseparable with her sisters Faye and Sharon, making up the singing group of the Henderson Sisters. The sisters have sang all over the country including Nassau, Bahamas and Mexico City. Coming from a loving family of God-fearing people, Bishop coney was inspired by her grandfather, the late Rev. H. C. Williams, former Pastor of the renowned Friendly Baptist Church of Philadelphia.

As a small child, she would sit at her grandfather's feet and sketch drawings of the sermons he prepared to deliver to his congregation. She still uses her creativity to design her own greeting cards and other miscellaneous craft items, under the name of Rosette's Creations. In June of 1971 Bishop Coney married Deacon Gene Coney. They are the proud parents of two daughters and sons in-law, two beautiful granddaughters, Makayla Rose and Tamia Camille; as well as a handsome young grandson, Aaron. They have many spiritual sons and daughters as well. Bishop and Deacon Coney reside in Glenside, PA.

Her spiritual work began at the House of God (Keith Dominion) then the Church of the Living God (Jewell Dominion) and has allowed her to work in leadership positions since childhood, serving in every possible office in the church from President of the Usher Board to her present position of Bishop and Pastor. Currently, Bishop Coney is leading a group of enthusiastic people in the Kensington section of the city of Philadelphia, where God has continued to grow the membership. Her personal accomplishments are too numerous to put in writing, and she gives God all the glory for what He has done through her.

Bishop Coney worked in the corporate world for 30 years, and has to her credit the gift of stability. In June of 1999 she graduated as valedictorian of the Trinity School of Enlightenment, and willingly followed the direction of the Holy Spirit to leave the corporate world to do full-time ministry work. She is an active member of the Bethel Deliverance International Fellowship of Churches in Philadelphia, PA, which allows her ministry experience to expand even further under the great tutelage of Bishop Eric A. Lambert. She is also a member of the Strawberry Mansion Faith Based Coalition. Bishop Coney is mentored by Dr. Faye Moore, General Overseer/Senior Bishop of the Church of the Living God, and Bishop Millicent Hunter, Senior Pastor of the Cathedral Baptist Worship Center. In 2013, Bishop Coney was the recipient of the prestigious "**Masters Award**" and honored at a formal banquet at the Enon Tabernacle Baptist Church. This honor is awarded to a Disciple of Christ who demonstrates strong Christian character, principles, values and morals in life, while fighting the forces of evil.

FOR SPEAKING ENGAGEMENTS AND FEEDBACK

PLEASE CONTACT BISHOP CONEY

267-258-8331

**OR VIA EMAIL
ROSETTECREATIONS@COMCAST.NET**

Take Your Feet Off The Seat